LET'S EXPLORE THE STATES

Atlantic

North Carolina
Virginia
West Virginia

Tish Davidson

Mason Crest
450 Parkway Drive, Suite D
Broomall, PA 19008
www.masoncrest.com

Printed and bound in the United States of America.

CPSIA Compliance Information: Batch #LES2015.
For further information, contact Mason Crest at 1-866-MCP-Book.

First printing
1 3 5 7 9 8 6 4 2

Library of Congress Cataloging-in-Publication Data

Davidson, Tish.
  Atlantic : North Carolina, Virginia, West Virginia / Tish Davidson.
      pages cm. — (Let's explore the states)
  Includes bibliographical references and index.
  ISBN 978-1-4222-3320-7 (hc)
  ISBN 978-1-4222-8605-0 (ebook)
  1. Atlantic States—Juvenile literature. 2. North Carolina—Juvenile literature.
  3. Virginia—Juvenile literature. 4. West Virginia—Juvenile literature. I. Title.
  F106.D256 2015
  975—dc23

                        2014050173

Let's Explore the States series ISBN: 978-1-4222-3319-1

About the Author: Tish Davidson has written many articles for newspapers and magazines. Her books for middle school readers include *African American Scientists and Inventors* and *Facing Competition*. Davidson graduated from the College of William and Mary and earned a master's degree from Dartmouth College. She lives in Fremont, California, and is a volunteer puppy raiser for Guide Dogs for the Blind.

Picture Credits: Action Sports Photography: 22 (bottom); Architect of the Capitol: 34; Library of Congress: 11, 12, 16, 17, 18, 22 (top left), 35, 36 (right), 54; National Aeronautics and Space Administration: 22 (top right); National Guard Heritage Collection: 36 (left); National Park Service: 14, 32; used under license from Shutterstock, Inc.: 5, 6, 7, 9, 10, 26, 27, 29, 30, 31, 39 (bottom), 41, 43, 44, 48, 49, 52, 58, 59; American Spirit / Shutterstock.com: 1, 19, 37, 51, 57; S. Bukley / Shutterstock.com: 39 (top), 42 (left); Helga Esteb / Shutterstock.com: 42 (top right), 60 (left); D. Free / Shutterstock.com: 42 (bottom right); Mavrick / Shutterstock.com: 38; Lissandra Melo / Shutterstock.com: 40; Bryan Pollard / Shutterstock.com: 21; StacieStauffSmith Photos / Shutterstock.com: 45; U.S. Naval Academy Museum Collection: 60 (right); U.S. Senate Collection: 56; The Woolaroc Museum: 15.

Table of Contents

KEY ICONS TO LOOK FOR:

 Text-dependent questions: These questions send the reader back to the text for more careful attention to the evidence presented there.

 Words to understand: These words with their easy-to-understand definitions will increase the reader's understanding of the text, while building vocabulary skills.

 Series glossary of key terms: This back-of-the book glossary contains terminology used throughout this series. Words found here increase the reader's ability to read and comprehend higher-level books and articles in this field.

 Research projects: Readers are pointed toward areas of further inquiry connected to each chapter. Suggestions are provided for projects that encourage deeper research and analysis.

 Sidebars: This boxed material within the main text allows readers to build knowledge, gain insights, explore possibilities, and broaden their perspectives by weaving together additional information to provide realistic and holistic perspectives.

LET'S EXPLORE THE STATES

Atlantic: North Carolina, Virginia, West Virginia

Central Mississippi River Basin: Arkansas, Iowa, Missouri

East South-Central States: Kentucky, Tennessee

Eastern Great Lakes: Indiana, Michigan, Ohio

Gulf States: Alabama, Louisiana, Mississippi

Lower Atlantic: Florida, Georgia, South Carolina

Lower Plains: Kansas, Nebraska

Mid-Atlantic: Delaware, District of Columbia, Maryland

Non-Continental: Alaska, Hawaii

Northern New England: Maine, New Hampshire, Vermont

Northeast: New Jersey, New York, Pennsylvania

Northwest: Idaho, Oregon, Washington

Rocky Mountain: Colorado, Utah, Wyoming

Southern New England: Connecticut, Massachusetts, Rhode Island

Southwest: New Mexico, Oklahoma, Texas

U.S. Territories and Possessions

Upper Plains: Montana, North Dakota, South Dakota

West: Arizona, California, Nevada

Western Great Lakes: Illinois, Minnesota, Wisconsin

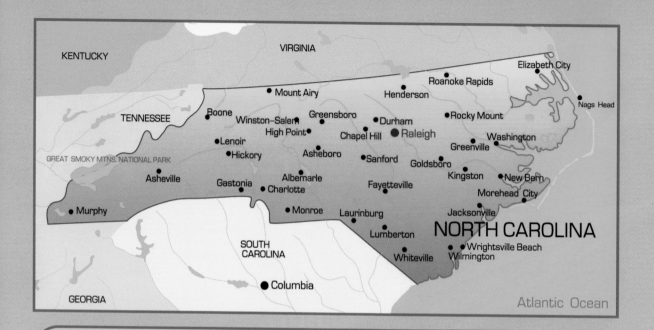

 ## North Carolina at a Glance

Area: 53,819 sq miles (139,391 sq km)[1]. (28th largest state)
  Land: 48,618 sq miles (78,243 sq km)
  Water: 5,201 sq miles (13,471 sq km)
Highest elevation: Mt. Mitchell, 6,684 feet (2,037 m)
Lowest elevation: Atlantic Ocean (sea level)

Statehood: November 1, 1789 (12th state)
Capital: Raleigh

Population: 9,943,964 (ninth largest state)[2]

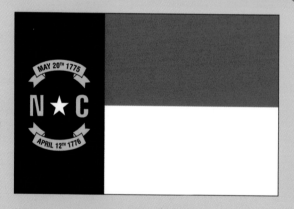

State nickname: Tarheel State
State bird: cardinal
State flower: American Dogwood

[1] *U.S. Census Bureau*
[2] *U.S. Census Bureau, 2014 estimate*

North Carolina

North Carolina has re-invented itself several times. It was given by the English king to private owners, and then bought back by a different king to become a British Colony. It was governed jointly with South Carolina, and then established a separate government. Later it joined South Carolina and ten other Southern states to form the Confederate States of America, only to rejoin the United States at the end of the Civil War.

Economically North Carolina has also changed greatly throughout its history. For more than 100 years it was a rural, agricultural state. It became a manufacturing state in the 20th century when textile mills in New England moved south. Once manufacturing jobs began moving overseas during the 1970s, North Carolina re-invented itself as a center for education, research, and finance. This ability to adapt and change to existing conditions gives North Carolina a bright future.

Geography

North Carolina is a southeastern state located in the middle of the Atlantic coast. It covers 53,819 square miles (139,391 sq km) and is the twenty-eighth largest state by land area. To the north, North Carolina shares a border with Virginia. Tennessee borders the state on the west, Georgia on the southwest, and South Carolina on the south. The Atlantic Ocean is on the east. North Carolina can be divided into three distinct geographic sections: the Coastal Plain, the Piedmont, and the Mountains.

The Coastal Plain covers about 45 percent of North Carolina. The Outer

Words to Understand in This Chapter

biotechnology—the use of living organisms such as bacteria to produce useful products.

blockade—to block a port or other transportation route so that goods and people cannot pass through.

cape—a large piece of land extending into the ocean.

carpetbagger—a northerner who moved to the South after the Civil War to exploit the South's weaknesses and make money.

electoral votes—although the people vote in a popular election for the president, the president is officially elected by electoral votes. The number of electoral votes for each state is equal to the total of its U.S. senators and representatives.

literacy test—a test that proves a person knows how to read and write. In the United States, it is now illegal to require a citizen to pass a literacy test to be able to vote.

pharmaceuticals—legal prescription and nonprescription drugs.

segregation—separation of a group of people based on their race, color, religion, sex, or national origin.

sound—a large body of water that separates two land masses.

textile—cloth or other products produced by knitting or weaving.

Wild horses graze in the dunes near beach houses in Corolla, on the Outer Banks.

Coastal Plain includes the Outer Banks, a series of low sandy barrier islands. Within the Outer Banks are three *capes*, Cape Hatteras, Cape Lookout, and Cape Fear. This area is known as the Graveyard of the Atlantic because so many shipwrecks have occurred here.

The Outer Banks separate the Atlantic Ocean from seven bodies of water called *sounds*. The two largest are Albemarle Sound and Pamlico Sound. The Roanoke and the Chowan Rivers empty into the Albemarle Sound, while the Pamlico and Neuse Rivers empty into the Pamlico Sound.

On the mainland, the Outer Coastal Plain is low, flat land with many wetlands areas. The Inner Coastal Plain is higher and drier. Here

A view of Lake Norman, the largest manmade body of fresh water located in North Carolina. It was created in the Piedmont region during the early 1960s when the Cowans Ford Dam was built. The lake covers more than 50 square miles (130 sq km).

the soil is rich and good for farming.

The Piedmont covers the middle third of the state. Low hills rise from about 300 feet (91 m) above sea level in the east to about 1,100 feet (335 m) in the west where the Mountain section begins. Most large cities in North Carolina are in the Piedmont.

The Mountain section has several different mountain ranges including the Brushy Mountains, the Blue Ridge Mountains, the Great Smoky Mountains, and the Uwharrie Mountains. Mount Mitchell in the Blue Ridge range is the highest peak east of the Mississippi River, at 6,684 feet (2,037 m). The Uwharrie Mountains are the lowest and easternmost mountains in the state. The Mountain region is mostly covered with forests.

The Coastal Plain and the Piedmont are hot and humid in summer. Winters are mild with occasional light snow. The average high temperature in Wilmington, a coastal city, is 90° Fahrenheit (32° Celsius) in July and 56°F (13°C) in January. The mountains are cooler in summer and sometimes receive heavy snow in winter. The average high in Asheville, a mountain city, is 83°F (28°C) in July and 46°F (8°C) in January. The coast receives about 45 inches (114 cm) of rain each year. The mountains receive about 50 inches (127 cm) of mixed rain and snow.

Severe weather is common in North Carolina. An average of 31 tornadoes rip through the state each year, usually in the spring. Tropical storms and hurricanes often bring heavy wind and rain to the coast several times each year, and intense thunderstorms are common across the state in summer.

History

Before the arrival of Europeans, about thirty Native American tribes lived in what is now North Carolina. Among the most important were the Cherokee in the western mountains, the Catawaba, on the border with South Carolina, the Tuscarora, the largest band in the eastern part of the state, and the Croatans, a small coastal tribe.

Explorers working for France and Spain visited North Carolina between 1524 and 1539, but did not stay. The English, however, were interested in

This statue of the English explorer Sir Walter Raleigh is located in North Carolina's capital city. Raleigh was an important figure in the English exploration and colonization of North America during the late 16th century.

settling the area. In 1584, Sir Walter Raleigh sent two ships to what is now North Carolina. The sailors claimed the land for England, spent several months exploring, met friendly Native Americans, and returned home. The

Baptism of Virginia Dare, the first child born to English parents in America. John White brought news of Virginia's birth when he returned to England in 1587, but by the time he returned in 1590 she had disappeared along with the rest of the Roanoke Island colonists.

next year, Raleigh sent men to found a colony on Roanoke Island in the Outer Banks. The settlers managed to anger the Native Americans who had previously been helpful. As a result, the colonists almost starved. By chance, Sir Francis Drake, the first Englishman to sail around the world, arrived with a fleet of ships and took most of the colonists back to England.

Despite these setbacks, in 1587 Raleigh sent another group of colonists to Roanoke Island under the leadership of John White. When White arrived, he found the few men who had not returned with Drake had died or disappeared. Things did not go well for the new colonists, either. They arrived too late to plant crops and mistakenly attacked a group of Croatans who were friendly to them.

White returned to England to get more supplies, but because England was at war with Spain, he was unable to return to Roanoke Island until 1590. When he got back, all the colonists had disappeared. The only clues left behind were the words "CROATAN" and "CRO" carved into trees. White was forced to return to England. Today we call this attempt at settlement the Lost Colony. No one knows whether the colonists starved, were killed, or went to live with friendly Native Americans.

In 1629, King Charles I of England gave a large piece of land, including what is now North and South Carolina, to Sir Robert Heath. Heath failed to send colonists to the land. A few English settlers moved in from Virginia, but the land remained mostly free of Europeans.

Finally, in 1663, King Charles II divided Heath's land among eight men called Lords Proprietors. Settlers arrived slowly, some bringing with them African slaves. By 1690, North Carolina had about 8,000 residents. The first permanent European town, Bath, was established in 1705. By 1712, North and South Carolina had developed separate governments.

Great Britain began buying back the land it had given the Lords Proprietors. By 1729, it had bought out all but one of the Lords. The last one gave up his rights to the colony in a land swap in 1744. North Carolina was now a British colony with a royal governor appointed by the king. By 1760, about 150,000 free people and 50,000 slaves lived in the colony.

Like people in the other colonies, North Carolinians grew unhappy with the control Great Britain had over their lives. Some colonists, called Loyalists, wanted North Carolina to remain a British colony, but most wanted independence. In 1775, they joined with the other colonists in fighting the Revolutionary War, which lasted until 1783.

The Battle of Moore's Creek Bridge in February 1776 was the first Revolutionary War battle to be fought

 ## Did You Know?

When the English province of Carolina was divided into North and South Carolina in 1729, the border was supposed to run straight along the 35th parallel. But sometimes nature got in the way, and surveyors guessed where the border should be, used boundary markers that were later destroyed, or simply gave up and stopped marking the border. Each of four surveys between 1813 and 1928 changed the border. In the early 1990s, a new survey was started. As of 2014, the governments of North and South Carolina were close to agreeing to a final state border. Some people will suddenly be living in a different state without ever moving!

The largest Revolutionary War battle in the South was fought in rural North Carolina, at Guilford Courthouse. Although the British were technically the victors, the army was so weakened that it had to abandon plans to attack the Continental Army in the Carolinas. Lord Cornwallis, the British commander, retreated to Virginia, where his army was trapped by George Washington at Yorktown.

in North Carolina. However, most of the fighting in North Carolina happened late in the war. In January 1781, General Nathanael Greene tricked the British under General Cornwallis into moving into North Carolina, separating them from their base in Charleston, South Carolina.

In March 1781, the armies of Greene and Cornwallis fought the battle of Guilford Courthouse near Greensboro. Although the Continental Army lost the battle, the British were severely weakened. Cornwallis was forced to surrender at Yorktown,

Virginia, on October 19, 1781, and the war ended.

North Carolina sent delegates to the Constitutional Convention in Philadelphia in 1787. At first, the delegates rejected the Constitution because they thought it gave too much power to the federal government and not enough to the states. After the addition of the first ten amendments to the Constitution known as the Bill of Rights, North Carolinians ratified the Constitution. On November 21, 1789, North Carolina became the twelfth state.

Between the Revolutionary War and the beginning of the Civil War (1861–1865), North Carolina was a rural state. Even though the state had miles of coastline, it had no good harbor and did not develop a strong trading economy. North Carolina remained agricultural and grew slowly. In 1860, the capital, Raleigh, had only 5,000 residents.

On the coast, plantations worked by slaves grew rice and tobacco. The small farms in the interior of the state grew grain and cotton, and in the mountains, settlers harvested timber to be made into lumber.

The discovery of gold in the south central part of the state in 1799 drew many people westward into land occupied by the Cherokee Nation. This increased conflict between the settlers and the Native Americans. In 1830, President Andrew Jackson signed the Indian Removal Act to force all Native Americans in the Southeast to move to a reservation in Oklahoma Territory.

During the winter of 1838-39, about 15,000 native people were forced to walk 1,200 miles to

During the 1830s, the U.S. government implemented policies that removed Native Americans from their homes in North Carolina and other states, and forced them to move to new lands in the west.

Oklahoma under terrible conditions. About 4,000 died along the way. Today this forced march is known as the Trail of Tears. Some Cherokees escaped and hid in the North Carolina mountains. Their descendants became the Eastern Band of Cherokees. This is the only federally recognized Native American tribe in North Carolina today.

In 1861, tensions between the northern and southern states over slavery came to a head. Several states led by South Carolina declared that

Union and Confederate soldiers battle for control of Fort Fisher near Wilmington. As long as the fort protected the harbor, blockade runners could bring supplies for the Confederacy into North Carolina. The fort was captured by the Union army in January 1865, a few months before the Civil War ended.

they were seceding from the Union. North Carolina was not one of the original seven, but when President Abraham Lincoln ordered North Carolina troops to fight against South Carolina, North Carolina seceded instead. It became the last of the eleven states that formed the Confederate States of America.

Few Civil War battles were fought in North Carolina, but the state supplied the Confederate Army with 125,000 troops. About one-third of these soldiers died. Not all state residents supported the Confederacy.

Free black North Carolinians, freed slaves, and several thousand whites from the western part of the state fought for the Union Army.

During the war, the Union Navy **blockaded** ports in southern states. In 1862, the Union took control of the Outer Banks, disrupting trade. This caused food riots and hardship in some North Carolina towns.

The period immediately after the Civil War is called Reconstruction. After the war ended, some northerners moved to the South to take economic advantage of the disruptions caused by the fighting. These northerners were called *carpetbaggers*. They were despised for exploiting the South's weakness.

North Carolina was readmitted to the Union in 1868, but many white residents were unwilling to treat African Americans as equals. They formed hate groups such as the Ku Klux Klan and the Red Shirts to terrorize black people and keep them from voting. They passed a new state constitution that made it difficult to register to vote, required voters to pay a poll tax, and required them to pass a *literacy test*. There followed a long period of suppression of African Americans' rights and enforcement of *segregation* in all public places.

World War I (1914–1918) gave a temporary boost to the North Carolina economy, but the Great Depression, which began in 1929, hurt the state's economy and left many people out of work. The economy improved during World War II (1941–1945), when North Carolina *textile* mills provided cloth for military uniforms. However, most residents of the state depended on agriculture for their living.

During the 1950s, North Carolina was a poor state with the second-low-

The first sustained and controlled heavier-than-air, powered flight occurred in North Carolina on December 17, 1903. Inventors Orville and Wilbur Wright chose to test their aircraft, called the "Wright Flyer," at Kill Devil Hills in the Outer Banks near Kitty Hawk, because the area was known for its steady, strong winds. The beaches there provided a clear area where they could launch the craft, and soft dunes where they could land safely.

An African-American man waits for a bus outside the "colored waiting room," 1940s. Segregation was the law throughout North Carolina for much of the 20th century, with blacks required to use separate restaurants, bus waiting rooms, drinking fountains, and even bathrooms.

est income per person in the nation. In response, the state sought to attract high-paying jobs in private industry. The state built the physical infrastructure to attract factories, and passed laws favorable to business. Money was poured into the state's schools to educate skilled workers. The result, Research Triangle Park, opened in 1959. Today it is the home of ***pharmaceutical***, research, and ***biotechnology*** companies. It is one of the most successful joint public-private economic transformations to have occurred in any state.

North Carolina was experiencing social as well as economic changes. In 1960 in Greensboro, four black students sat down to peacefully protest segregation at Woolworth's whites-only lunch counter. Protests against segregation spread, in North Carolina and elsewhere. In 1964, a federal law known as the Civil Rights Act prohibited discrimination on the basis of race, color, religion, sex, or national origin. Slowly, and with occasional violence, the state moved to integrate its schools, restaurants, hotels, and other public places.

Like many states, in the 1980s and 1990s North Carolina lost manufacturing jobs to foreign countries where labor costs were lower. Sales of tobacco, the state's main crop, also declined due to anti-smoking campaigns. But while agriculture remains a major part of the state's economy, North Carolina has been successful in improving its educational system and attracting advanced technology and research companies giving the state a solid future.

Government

North Carolina is governed from the capital, Raleigh. The current constitution was written in 1971. The state's government is patterned after the federal government with executive, legislative, and judicial branches. The executive branch of government in North Carolina is larger than in many states. It consists of a governor, lieutenant governor, and a Council of State to advise the governor. All positions are elected statewide every four years.

Positions on the Council of State

A monument to fallen Confederate soldiers rises 75 feet (23 m) above the ground of North Carolina's state capitol building in Raleigh. The governor's office is located in the capitol building; the state assembly meets in a nearby legislative building that was opened in 1963.

are secretary of state, state auditor, state treasurer, superintendent of public instruction, attorney general, commissioner of labor, commissioner of agriculture, and commissioner of insurance. The governor also appoints the heads of as many as 25 different government departments. The governor and lieutenant governor can serve only two terms in a row. Members of the Council of State can be re-elected without term limits.

The General Assembly consists of two houses, the Senate with 50 members and the House of Representatives with 120 members. Elections for all General Assembly members are held every two years. On odd number years, the General Assembly meets for what is called the long session, which lasts about six months. On even number years, the Assembly meets for a short session of about six weeks.

The judicial branch is headed by the State Supreme Court. Its seven justices are elected by the public for eight-year terms. The Supreme Court hears only cases involving questions of legal procedure or interpretation of laws. The Court of Appeals was created in 1967. Its fifteen judges are chosen in statewide elections and serve eight-year terms. Like the Supreme Court, this court hears only questions of law, not of guilt or innocence. Cases are heard by a three-judge panel.

Major violations of the law (felonies) and those involving large amounts of money are heard in Superior Court, while minor violations of the law (misdemeanors), cases involving lesser amounts of money, and cases involving family relationships are heard in District Courts.

North Carolina sends two senators and thirteen representatives to the Congress in Washington, DC, giving it fifteen electoral votes.

The Economy

From the time North Carolina was first settled until the early 1900s, it was almost exclusively an agricultural state. Beginning in the early 1900s, textile manufacturers began moving their factories from New England to the South. North Carolina factories began producing cloth, furniture, and cigarettes. Even with all this activity, North Carolina remained a relatively poor state through the 1950s.

In the 1970s and 1980s, manufacturing companies began moving their factories out of North Carolina to locations overseas. The state responded by developing business-university partnerships to attract research and service businesses. Research Triangle Park in the Raleigh-Durham-Chapel Hill area developed from this effort.

The park is anchored by three major universities. In 2014, it had over 170 companies that employ 40,000 people. Many of these companies are involved in pharmaceutical or biotechnology research and manufacturing. Similar business-university partnerships have been developed near Winston-Salem, Charlotte, Greensboro, and Kannapolis. In 2014, North Carolina ranked tenth in the nation in manufacturing.

North Carolina has the third largest military population in the United States. The Army's Fort Bragg one of the largest bases in the world.

Today, 12 percent of all jobs in North Carolina are related to servicing the military.

Charlotte has become a powerful banking and financial services center. Tourism, education, and government also employ a larger number of North Carolinians.

Agriculture continues to be an important part of the state's economy with over 50,000 farms in the state today. Major crops include tobacco, sweet potatoes, corn, soybeans, peanuts, and cotton. The state also produces a large number of beef cattle, hogs, turkeys, chickens, and eggs.

The Reynolds American Building in Winston-Salem is the headquarters of R.J. Reynolds Tobacco Co., one of the largest cigarette companies in the United States. Since 1998, R.J. Reynolds and other major tobacco companies in North Carolina have made annual payments to state governments meant to cover some of the expenses of medical treatment for smokers.

Some Famous North Carolinians

Three presidents of the United States were born in North Carolina. Andrew Jackson (1767–1845), the seventh president, was born somewhere close to the border between North and South Carolina. James Polk (1797–1849), the eleventh president, was born in Pineville. Andrew Johnson (1808–1875), who became the seventeenth president after Abraham Lincoln was killed, was born in Raleigh.

Andrew Johnson

Wilbur (1867–1912) and Orville Wright (1871–1948), are strongly associated with North Carolina, even though they were Midwesterners. At Kitty Hawk on the Outer Banks on December 17, 1903, the brothers flew the first successful airplane a distance of 120 feet (37 m) at about ten feet above the ground. Sixty-nine years later, Charlotte native Charlie Duke (b. 1935) became the tenth man to walk on the moon during NASA's Apollo 16 mission.

Charlie Duke

Music has always been part of North Carolina's heritage. Many music stars come from the state including Tori Amos (b. 1963), Eric Church (b. 1983), Bucky Covington (b. 1977), Roberta Flack (b. 1937), Ben Folds (b. 1966), James Taylor (b. 1948), and Doc Watson (1923–2012). Clay Aiken (b. 1978), second place winner on *American Idol* in 2002, interrupted a successful music career to run for the U.S. House of Representatives in 2014.

NASCAR is popular in North Carolina. The state has produced two famous father-and-son drivers. Lee Petty (1914–2000) was a stock car driver and early NASCAR driver. His son, Richard Petty (b. 1937) had 200 NASCAR victories. Dale Earnhardt Sr. (1951–2001) won 76 NASCAR races before he was killed in a crash. His son, Dale Earnhardt Jr. (b. 1974), has followed in his father's winning footsteps.

Dale Earnhardt Jr.

The People

In the census of 1800, North Carolina had about 478,100 people including 133,300 slaves. By 2015, the population had reached 9,950,000, making North Carolina the ninth most populous state in the nation. About 7.5 percent of North Carolinians were born in a foreign country, and only 10.8 percent speak a language other than English at home compared to 20.5 percent of the nation as a whole.

In 2013, almost 72 percent of the population self-identified as white, but this included nearly 9 percent who also identify as Latino or Hispanic. The national average for Latino/Hispanic residents is 17.1 percent. Blacks made up 22 percent of the population compared to 13.2 percent in the nation as a whole.

Much smaller minorities include Asians (2.6 percent), Native Americans (1.6 percent), and those who identify with two or more races (2 percent).

North Carolinians are slightly less religious than people in the nation as a whole (48 percent vs. 49 percent).

Those who practice a religion are overwhelmingly Christian. The largest denomination is Baptist (19 percent), followed by Methodists (9 percent). Another 19.3 percent belong to other Christian churches. Less than 2 percent practice non-Christian religions.

People in North Carolina graduate from high school (84.5 percent) and earn college degrees (26.8 percent) at rates only slightly lower than the national average.

Despite success in bringing some well-paying jobs to the state, the median household income between 2008 and 2012 was $46,450, about $7,000 less than the national average. During this same period, 16.8 percent of the population had incomes below the federal poverty level.

Major Cities

Charlotte, located in the western Piedmont region near the South Carolina border, is North Carolina's largest city and the sixteenth largest city in the United States. In 2014, it had about 793,000 residents. The city is a major financial center and headquarters of Bank of America. Charlotte has two major league sports teams, the Carolina Panthers of the National Football League and the Charlotte Hornets of the National Basketball Association. The city is also a center for NASCAR racing and home to the NASCAR Hall of Fame.

Raleigh is named after Sir Walter Raleigh, who tried to establish a colony on Roanoke Island in the 16th century. It is North Carolina's second-largest city and the state capital. Raleigh is home to North Carolina State University. It is part of the Research Triangle Park area along with *Durham*, home of Duke University and *Chapel Hill*, home of the University of North Carolina.

Greensboro, the third-largest city in the state, is located in the north central Piedmont region where three interstate highways meet. The city has always depended heavily on the manufacturing of textiles, tobacco products, and furniture. More recently, it has become a center for the heavy truck production, while expanding non-manufacturing industries such as insurance and banking.

In the western part of the state *Asheville* is the largest city near Great Smoky Mountain National Park. The park's main entrance in North Carolina is at Cherokee. On the Atlantic Coast, *Nags Head* serves as a gateway to Cape Hatteras National Seashore.

Further Reading

Burgan, Michael. *African Americans in the Thirteen Colonies*. New York: Children's Press, 2013.

Golay, Michael. *Civil War*, revised ed. New York: Chelsea House, 2011.

Heinrichs, Ann. *North Carolina*. New York: Children's Press, 2009.

Marsh, Carol. *The Mystery of the Graveyard of the Atlantic*. Peachtree City, Ga.: Gallopade International, 2011.

Zepke, Terrance. *Pirates of the Carolinas for Kids*. Sarasota, Fla.: Pineapple Press, 2009.

Internet Resources

http://www.thrivenc.com/keyindustries/overview>

Information about the major industries in North Carolina from the state's department of commerce.

http://www.northcarolinahistory.org

An online encyclopedia of North Carolina history with lesson plans and commentary.

http://www.history.ncdcr.gov

The North Carolina Office of Archives and History provides links to primary sources in the state archives and to other state historical associations.

http://www.secretary.state.nc.us/kidspg/history.htm

The North Carolina Secretary of State Kids' History Page includes a timeline of important events in North Carolina's history from before human habitation.

http://www.visitnc.com

The official travel and tourism site of the state of North Carolina.

 # Text-Dependent Questions

1. What are the characteristics of the three major geographic areas in North Carolina?
2. Why did the North Carolina's delegates to the Constitutional Convention in Philadelphia object the new U.S. Constitution? What made them change their minds?
3. How is the economy of North Carolina different now from the way it was in 1900?

 # Research Project

Read about the Lost Colony on Roanoke Island. Write a few paragraphs on the problems the colonists faced and what you think might have happened to them when they disappeared.

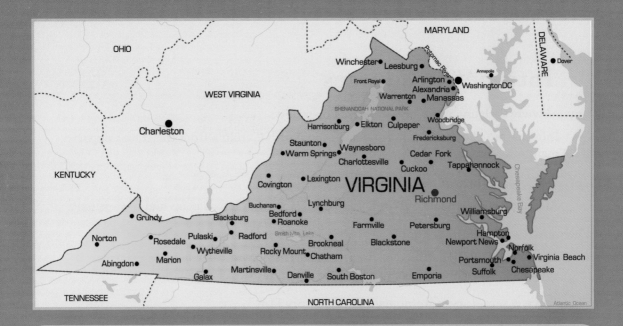

 Virginia at a Glance

Area: 42,775 sq mi (110,787 sq km)[1]
   (35th largest state)
   Land: 39,490 sq mi (102,279 sq km)
   Water: 3,285 sq mi (8,508 sq km)
Highest elevation: Mount Rogers,
   5,729 feet (1,609 m)
Lowest elevation: Atlantic Ocean,
   sea level

Statehood: June 25, 1788
   (10th state)
Capital: Richmond

Population: 8,326,289
   (12th largest state)[2]

State nickname: Old Dominion
State bird: cardinal
State flower: flowering dogwood

[1] *U.S. Census Bureau*
[2] *U.S. Census Bureau, 2014 estimate*

Virginia

Virginia may have more history per square mile than any other state. It was the site of the first permanent English colony in America, as well as the first elected legislature. As one of the original thirteen colonies, Virginians supported the Revolutionary War and helped to establish a new nation. Later they fought in a war that divided that country. Drive a few miles in any direction and you will likely encounter a Civil War battlefield. Virginians are proud of their history and equally proud of their present-day achievements.

Geography

Virginia, in the middle of the Atlantic coast, covers 42,755 square miles (110,787 sq km) and is the 35th-largest state in the nation. The state is shaped roughly like a triangle with an extended tip on the southwest. To the south, Virginia shares a border with North Carolina except at the southwest point. Here Virginia is bordered on the south by Tennessee and on the northwest for a short distance by Kentucky. Farther northwest, Virginia shares a border with West Virginia. At the northern point of the triangle, Virginia is separated from Maryland and the District of Columbia by the Potomac River.

The Chesapeake Bay forms most of the state's eastern border. It also isolates a small piece of Virginia from the rest of the state. This small peninsula is called the Eastern Shore. To the west of the Eastern Shore lies the Atlantic Ocean. The Bay is a large estuary. More than 150 rivers and stream flow into it including four major Virginia rivers, the Potomac, Rappahannock, York, and James.

Virginia is divided into five land areas. From east to west they are the Coastal Plain, also called Tidewater,

Words to Understand in This Chapter

Commonwealth—meaning "for the common good," in the United States it is the same as a state. Massachusetts, Pennsylvania, Virginia, and Kentucky all identify themselves as commonwealths.

confiscate—to take away private property for public or government use, often without payment.

desegregation—elimination of practices that keep different races separate in public spaces.

estuary—a place where freshwater rivers meet saltwater.

nursery plants—plants usually started in greenhouses and sold to landscapers and gardeners.

poverty level—the level of income below which a person or family is declared poor by government standards.

poll tax—a tax each adult has to pay in order to vote. Poll taxes can be used to keep poor or minority individuals from voting.

ratify—to formally approve a document such as a treaty or the Constitution.

secede—to withdraw; specifically for a state to leave the United States.

The Coleman Bridge crosses the York River near Yorktown in the Tidewater region.

View of the Blue Ridge Mountains from Shenandoah National Park.

Piedmont, Blue Ridge, Valley and Ridge, and in the far southwest, the Appalachian Plateau.

The Coastal Plain includes the land along the Chesapeake Bay including the Eastern Shore. It extends inland about 100 miles (160 km). The Coastal Plain is near sea level and has many flat, swampy areas.

West of the Coastal Plain, the Piedmont stretches across most of central Virginia, becoming broader as one travels from north to south. Here the land rises in low rolling hills. Where the land has not been cleared for farming, it is covered with forests.

Beyond the Piedmont, the Blue Ridge is a range of mountains that

Hills and farmland in Virginia's Piedmont region.

The Shenandoah River flows through Virginia and West Virginia. The river is the main tributary of the Potomac River, and is 56 miles (90 km) long.

runs from north to south following the western curve of the state. The highest point in Virginia, Mount Rogers, is in the Blue Ridge. Soil here is thin and rocky and not good for farming.

West of the Blue Ridge, a series of parallel valleys are separated by lower mountains. This is the Valley and Ridge region. The Shenandoah Valley, the largest of the valleys, has good soil and many farms. This area is known for its scenic beauty and its limestone caves. It attracts hikers, cave explorers, and outdoor enthusiasts.

The Appalachian Plateau occupies the southwest tip of Virginia and extends into Kentucky. It is a series of forest-covered flat land separated by steep valleys. Coal mining is an important main industry here.

The climate of Virginia varies depending on location. The Coastal Plain is warm, humid, and rarely gets snow. The region does occasionally get high winds and heavy rain from tropical storms and hurricanes. In Norfolk, the average temperature throughout the year ranges from 34°F (1°C) in January to 88°F (31°C) in July.

Moving west, the climate becomes slightly cooler and less humid. The coldest weather occurs in the mountains where snow is common. The western part of the state is occasionally struck by tornadoes. The average temperature in Blacksburg ranges from 24°F (–4°C) in January to 84°F (29°C) in July.

History

Before Europeans arrived, many Native Americans lived in Virginia. The Powhatan, who lived on the Coastal Plain, were a group of more than 30 tribes that spoke the Algonquian language and shared certain customs. At the time European settlers arrived, these tribes were united under a powerful chief named Wahunsunacock. Settlers would later encounter Monacan and Moneton tribes in the central part of the state and Cherokee in the Appalachian Plateau.

Jamestown, founded in May 1607, was site of the first permanent English settlement in America. Some of the settlers spent their time hunting for gold (there was none) instead of planting crops and building homes. John Smith, a young colonist, took charge and forced the people to work. Even so, two-thirds of the colonists died of disease, accidents, and starvation

Colonists construct a fort at Jamestown, the first permanent English settlement in North America, in 1607. Jamestown was abandoned in 1699, when the capital of Virginia was moved to Williamsburg. Today, archaeologists continue to learn more about life in colonial America through excavations at the site on the Virginia peninsula.

within the first year. The colony probably would not have survived without the help of Wahunsunacock and the Powhatan.

More colonists arrived from England, but the situation did not improve. The winter of 1609–1610 was called "the starving time." In the autumn, the colony had 500 settlers. By spring 60 were left. They were saved only by the arrival of ships bringing supplies from England.

Jamestown would have continued to struggle if it had not been for tobacco, which grew well in Jamestown. John Rolfe, a colonist who later married Wahunsunacock's daughter, Pocahontas, figured out how to dry tobacco leaves and ship them to Europe. In Europe, tobacco was a high-priced luxury. Soon colonists became wealthy selling tobacco.

In 1619, 1,200 new colonists arrived in Virginia ready to make their fortunes. At this time, Jamestown was ruled by a governor appointed in England. The governor made all the laws. As more colonists arrived, they wanted a voice in how the settlement

 Did You Know?

The College of William and Mary in Williamsburg is the second-oldest college in the United States. The College's Wren Building is the oldest classroom building in the nation that is still in use. The building also served as a temporary meeting place for the House of Burgesses and as a Confederate hospital during the Civil War.

was run. In July 1619, landowning colonists created the House of Burgesses, the first elected legislative body in America. The House could pass new laws, but the governor could veto them.

Growing tobacco in Jamestown required a lot of land and a lot of labor. The first African slaves arrived in the colony in 1619 to work in the tobacco fields. Native Americans were also captured and forced to work. In 1622, frustrated by colonists stealing their land and their people, Native Americans killed about 350 settlers. But more slaves and more colonists kept coming.

The Revolution ended after the Continental Army, commanded by Virginian George Washington, trapped a British army led by General Charles Cornwallis on the Virginia peninsula and forced him to surrender at Yorktown on October 19, 1781. This painting depicts Cornwallis's surrender to Washington, who is mounted on horseback. The British defeat at Yorktown marked the end of the fighting, but a peace treaty between the United States and Great Britain was not signed until 1783.

Large tobacco plantations grew up along the James River. On these plantations, a few white families lived in luxury while slaves worked the land. This pattern of colonization was different from New England where tradesmen live close together in towns and families worked small farms nearby.

By the early 1700s, the American colonies were resentful of British rule. They particularly hated the taxes the British made them pay. Rebellion was in the air. Patrick Henry gave a passionate speech to the House of Burgesses urging Virginians to support war with Great Britain. He ended his speech with the famous line "give me liberty or give me death." After this speech, the House of Burgesses decided to support the war.

In April 1775, citizens of Massachusetts fought British troops at Lexington and Concord. The Revolutionary War had begun. The next year, Thomas Jefferson, a Virginian, wrote the Declaration of Independence. Virginia sent men north to fight, and military leaders like George Washington, Daniel Morgan,

"Light House" Harry Lee, and George Rodgers Clark played a key role in many important battles.

After the war ended in 1783, Virginians played a major role in founding the new nation. James Madison wrote most of the Constitution, which Virginia ratified to became the tenth state on June 25, 1788. Four of the first five American presidents came from Virginia: Washington, Jefferson, Madison, and James Monroe.

After statehood, many settlers moved west into the Piedmont Region and later into the Valley and Ridge region. The land in the west was not suited to large plantations. Instead, the settlers worked small farms where they raised some cotton, corn, wheat, hogs, cattle, and sheep.

During this time, plantation owners on the Coastal Plain depended on slave labor to support their lifestyle. Most cities had a slave market. Richmond's was one of the largest in the country.

The slave trade caused tensions between North and South, but it also

Soldiers stand outside a slave market in Alexandria, circa 1861. The issue of slavery divided the country, leading to a civil war between the northern and southern states.

caused divisions within Virginia. The small farmers who moved west worked the land themselves or with only a few slaves. They did not depend on slave labor the way the Coastal Plain plantation owners did. This difference created a division between the poorer western farmers and the rich plantation owners.

Eventually, tensions between the North and South boiled over. South Carolina was the first state to secede from the Union on December 20, 1860. Powerful plantation owners and other Virginians who depended on slave labor were in favor of joining the states that had seceded and formed the Confederate States of America. The western counties of Virginia, where slavery was less important, wanted to stay in the Union.

Virginia was bitterly divided. The state voted to join the Confederacy five days after the first shots of the Civil War were fired at Fort Sumter in South Carolina in April 1861. But the western Virginia counties rejected the vote to secede. Instead, they voted to leave Virginia and create West Virginia as a separate state that would remain in the Union. A series of legal maneuvers began. After West Virginia agreed to abolish slavery, it separated from Virginia and was admitted to the United States on June 20, 1863.

Virginia was the backbone of the Confederacy. Richmond was the Confederate capital, and Virginia was

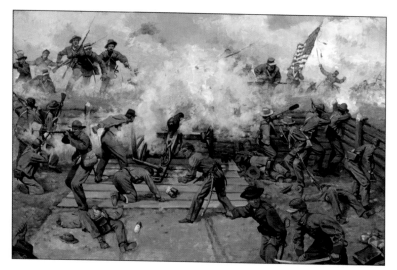

Virginia was the site of many battles during the Civil War. (Left) Union troops overrun a Confederate fort during the siege of Petersburg, 1864. (Right) General Robert E. Lee surrenders the Army of Northern Virginia to Union commander Ulysses S. Grant at Appomatox Court House, April 1865. Although some Confederate forces continued to fight for a few months, Lee's surrender ended Confederate hopes of a successful revolution.

the Confederacy's most industrialized state. The state quickly became a major battleground. About 2,200 Civil War battles were fought in the Virginia. In addition to the 620,000 or more soldiers who died in the war, ordinary people had their lives upended when either army swept through an area *confiscating* horses, livestock, and grain or burning anything they thought might help the other side.

The war dragged on for four years until General Robert E. Lee surrendered his Confederate Army in Virginia at Appomattox Court House on April 9, 1865. Most Confederate soldiers were allowed to return home without punishment, but by this time, much of the South was in ruins. Many of them had little to return to.

The period immediately following the Civil War is known as Reconstruction. This was a period of great bitterness. African Americans were granted citizenship and equal protection under the law in 1868 by the fourteenth amendment to the Constitution, but southern whites continued find ways to restrict their

An estate owned by the family of Confederate General Robert E. Lee was seized during the Civil War and used as a cemetery for Union soldiers. Today, Arlington National Cemetery is the final resting place for soldiers who served in many of America's confilcts.

freedom. A military government took over much of the South until Reconstruction formally ended in 1870 when Virginia wrote a new constitution and was re-admitted to the Union.

Virginia was back in the Union, but many of its citizens were determined to hold African Americans to second-class status. State legislators passed laws, known as Jim Crow Laws, that forced the races be kept separate on public transportation, in schools, restaurants, and in housing. Poll taxes and threats of violence kept African Americans from voting.

This situation began to change with the 1954 case *Brown v. Board of Education*, in which the U. S. Supreme Court ruled that racially segregated schools were illegal. Still many

In January 2015, former Virginia governor Bob McDonnell and his wife, Maureen, were convicted of federal corruption charges. While in office, they had received improper gifts and loans from a Virginia businessman. McDonnell, the first Virginia governor to be convicted of a felony, was sentenced to two years in prison.

Virginia school districts fought the law. The Civil Rights Act signed by President Lyndon Johnson in 1964 prohibited discrimination based on race, color, religion, or national origin. The law also provided the federal government with the powers to enforce *desegregation*.

Change came slowly to Virginia, but over time, the effects of the Civil Rights Act could be seen in schools, restaurants, hospitals, and in politics. In 1990, L. Douglas Wilder was elected governor of Virginia, the first African American governor in the United States. And during the 2012 presidential election, a majority of Virginians voted for Barack Obama.

Government

The *Commonwealth* of Virginia is governed from Richmond. Richmond is Virginia's third capital. The first two were Jamestown and then Williamsburg. The state constitution follows the organization of the U. S. Constitution with three branches of state government: executive, legislative, and judicial.

The executive branch consists of the governor, lieutenant governor, and attorney general. These officials are elected to four-year terms. The governor may serve only one term in a row, although he or she may be re-elected after sitting out at least one term. The lieutenant governor may serve back-to-back terms. The governor and lieutenant governor run separately, so it is possible to have a governor elected from one party and a lieutenant governor from a different party.

Virginia's legislative branch is known as the General Assembly. It began in 1619 as the House of Burgesses and is the oldest continuously functioning law-making body in the United States. The General Assembly has two houses. The Senate has 40 members who are elected to four-year terms. The House of

In 2014, Terry McAuliffe became governor of Virginia.

The Virginia State Capitol houses the state assembly. The building in Richmond was constructed in the 1780s, although two wings were added to the building in the early 20th century. In 2007, a major project to renovate and restore the building was finished.

Delegates has 100 members who are elected to two-year terms.

The Supreme Court is the highest court in Virginia. The seven justices are elected by both houses of the General Assembly and serve twelve-year terms. Under the Supreme Court are the Court of Appeal, Circuit Courts, and District Courts.

Virginia sends two Senators and eleven Representatives to Washington to represent the state in Congress. This gives Virginia thirteen electoral votes in presidential elections.

The Economy

Before the Civil War, Virginia's economy was built on agriculture. After the war, Virginia, like much of the South, had to rebuild its economy almost from scratch. Today the state has a diverse economy in which agriculture

Each year, thousands of people visit Mount Vernon, the plantation home of George Washington.

The Pentagon in Arlington is the headquarters of the U.S. Department of Defense, which oversees all American military operations.

plays only a small role.

In 2013, government was the largest employer in the Virginia. Nineteen percent of all workers were government employees. Government workers are concentrated in two places. In Arlington County outside Washington, DC, the Pentagon, home of the Department of Defense, employs approximately 30,000 peo- ple. The Office of Naval Research, the National Science Foundation, the Transportation Security Agency, and many other federal government agencies have offices in or near Arlington County.

Hampton Roads, made up of the cities of Norfolk, Virginia Beach, Newport News, and Chesapeake also has many government employees.

Some Famous Virginians

Virginia has produced many people who have influenced the history of the United States. Eight U.S. Presidents—George Washington, Thomas Jefferson, James Madison, James Monroe, William Henry Harrison, John Tyler, Zachary Taylor, and Woodrow Wilson—came from Virginia. So have nine Supreme Court Justices.

But Virginia has more than famous historical figures. The state has produced stars in almost every major sport. Tennis player Arthur Ashe (1943–1993) of Richmond was the first African American to be chosen for the U.S. Davis Cup team and became the number one ranked tennis player in the world. Lawrence Taylor (b. 1959) from Williamsburg, the National Football League Hall of Fame line-backer, played his entire career for the New York Giants, retiring in 1993. Alonzo Mourning (b. 1970) of Chesapeake had a 15-year career in the National Basketball Association. He was inducted into the Basketball Hall of Fame in 2014. Olympian Gabby Douglas (b. 1995) from Virginia Beach at age 16 became the first American gymnast to win a gold medal in both the individual all-around and team competitions at the same Olympics.

Gabby Douglas

The field of music has also been enriched by many talented Virginians. Maybelle Carter (1909–1978) and her daughter June Carter Cash (1929–2003) came from rural backgrounds to become country music stars. Ella Fitzgerald (1917–1996) of Newport News was queen of the jazz world. More recently, multi-talented Pharrell

Pharrell Williams

Williams (b. 1973) from Virginia Beach, a singer-songwriter, rapper, record producer, and fashion designer, became an international star with his hit song "Happy."

Sandra Bullock

Among the notable actors from Virginia are Sandra Bullock (b. 1964 in Arlington), who won an Academy Award in 2010. Rob Lowe (b. 1964 in Charlottesville) has starred in many hit movies and TV shows.

More than 60,000 active duty military members are stationed at the Norfolk Naval Station, the largest naval base in the world. Shipbuilding and repair, along with other support services for the military, play a major role in the region's economy.

Across the state, other areas of employment include professional and business services (18 percent of workers), trade, transportation, and utilities (17 percent), education and healthcare (13 percent), and leisure and hospitality (10 percent). This gives the state a, balanced economy. Coal mining is important in the southwestern part of the state. Fishing, crabbing, and oyster farming provide employment in coastal areas. Major farm products are greenhouse and nursery plants, soybeans, tobacco, apples, chickens, and turkeys.

The city of Norfolk has been an important port since the colonial era. It is located on the Elizabeth River.

Between 2008 and 2012, the median household income in Virginia was $63,636, about $10,000 higher than the national average. However, during this same period, 11.1 percent of residents' incomes fell below the poverty level.

The People

According to the census of 1800, 676,682 people lived in what is now Virginia. This included 322,199 slaves, just under half the population. In 2013, the population had grown to about 8.2 million. Virginia is the twelfth most populous state in the nation.

About 11 percent of Virginians were born in a foreign country, and almost 15 percent speak a language other than English at home. This compares to the national average of 12.9

Arlington County is located across the Potomac River from Washington, D.C. The population is 227,000, making it the fourth-largest municipality in Virginia.

Colonial Williamsburg is a unique living history museum located in the historic city of Williamsburg. The district includes many buildings constructed between 1699 and 1780, when Williamsburg was the capital of Virginia.

percent foreign-born residents and 20.5 percent of people who speak another home language.

In 2013, 63 percent of the population self-identified as white and 8 percent as Hispanic or Latino. Blacks or African Americans made up 20 percent of the population. About 6 percent self-identified as Asian, and 2.7 percent identified with two or more races.

Virginians are slightly less religious than people in the nation as a whole (45 percent vs. 49 percent). Latter Day Saints (Mormons) make up 12 percent of those who say they actively practice a religion. They are the largest denomination in the state. About 9 percent of the religious population is Roman Catholic, and 20.5 percent belong to all other Christian churches. About 2.7 percent of the religious population is Muslim, while Muslims make up less than 1 percent of the religiously active population in the nation.

Major Cities

The Hampton Roads area in southeast Virginia is made up of the state's three largest cities, **Virginia Beach**, **Norfolk**, and **Chesapeake**, along with its sixth-largest city, **Newport News**. Hampton Roads has one of the world's great natural harbors, making Norfolk a Navy town. The world's largest naval base is located here. **Virginia Beach** is a resort town with miles of Atlantic beaches. Every year the East Coast Surfing Championships are held here.

Richmond, the current capital, was also the capital of the Confederacy during the Civil War. The capitol building was designed by Thomas Jefferson. It was completed in 1788 and is still used today. Richmond is the home of many museums, including the Virginia Historical Society, the Virginia Museum of Fine Arts, and the Science Museum of Virginia.

Williamsburg is best known for Colonial Williamsburg, an active living history museum incorporated into the city. Costumed historic re-enactors demonstrate crafts, explain everyday life, and give tours of restored and reconstructed buildings from colonial times. Every year more than 4 million tourists come to visit this town. Many of them also visit nearby **Jamestown** and **Yorktown**.

Further Reading

Espinosa, Rod. *Patrick Henry*. Edina, MN: Magic Wagon, 2008.

Gillis, Jennifer Blizin. *The Confederate Soldier*. Minneapolis: Compass Point Books, 2007.

Golay, Michael. *Civil War*. Rev. ed. New York: Chelsea House, 2011.

Jerome, Kate Boehm. *Richmond and the State of Virginia: Cool Stuff Every Kid Should Know*. Mount Pleasant, SC: Arcadia Publishing, 2011.

Kent, Deborah. *Virginia*. New York: Children's Press, 2009.

Internet Resources

www.vahistorical.org/read-watch-listen/video-and-audio

The Virginia Historical Society provides an extensive selection of online video lectures covering all periods of Virginia history as well as topics of special historical interest. Also links to teachers' guides and primary sources.

www.americanheritage.com/travel/virginia

The American Heritage Travel Guide to Historic Sites in Virginia lists sites by category, with links to each site's webpage.

www.virginia.org

The official tourism website of the Commonwealth of Virginia.

www.civilwar.org

The Civil War Trust is a non-profit organization devoted to preserving Civil War battlefields. The website contains general information about the war and specific information about individual battles.

 # Text-Dependent Questions

1. What was the importance of tobacco to the colonists at Jamestown?
2. Why did West Virginia split off from Virginia and become a separate state?
3. Who is the largest employer in Virginia?

 # Research Project

More than 2,000 Civil War battles were fought in Virginia. Research one of these battles and write several paragraphs about what it would be like to be either a Confederate or a Union soldier at this battle.

West Virginia at a Glance

Area: 24,230 sq mi (62,755 sq km).[1]
(41st largest state)
Land: 24,038 sq mi (62,259 sq km)
Water: 192 sq mi (497 sq km)
Highest elevation: Spruce Knob,
4,861 feet (1482 m)
Lowest elevation: Potomac River at
Virginia border, 240 feet (73 m)

Statehood: June 20, 1863 (35th state)
Capital: Charleston

Population: 1,850,326
(38th largest state)[2]

State nickname: Mountain State
State bird: cardinal
State flower: rhododendron

*[1] Measurements of West Virginia vary; the
figure used is from the official state website.
[2] U.S. Census Bureau, 2014 estimate*

West Virginia

The development of West Virginia was strongly influenced by its geography. West Virginia was part of Virginia, but mountains were a barrier between it and the rest of the state. West Virginians developed their own identity, and by the Civil War, they were no longer content to be governed from distant Richmond. The tough, independent people of the mountains separated from Virginia and founded their own state in 1863.

Geography

West Virginia is an inland state in the central part of the eastern United States. It is shaped roughly like a shopping bag with two handles. The handles point north and east. The state covers about 24,030 square miles (62,700 square kilometers). The exact area of West Virginia is uncertain because until relatively recently Virginia and West Virginia were still squabbling over the boundaries between the states. The land is mostly mountainous.

West Virginia shares a long eastern and southern border with Virginia. The Ohio

River marks West Virginia's western border with Ohio, and the Big Sandy and Tug Fork Rivers form its western border with Kentucky. To the north, the state is bordered by Pennsylvania and Maryland.

West Virginia contains three land regions. In the east, the Appalachian Ridge and Valley region consists of a small strip of parallel valleys running from northeast to southwest separated and by ridges. Here the soil supports farming.

The Allegheny Mountains are west of the Ridge and Valley region. These mountains follow the border between Virginia and West Virginia and are the highest mountains in the state. The Monongahela National Forest covers a large section of this region.

West of the Allegheny Mountains lies the Appalachian Plateau. It covers about 80 percent of West Virginia. Here flat high land is separated by deep valleys. The Appalachian Plateau is the center of coal mining in West Virginia.

Because the mountains were barriers to building roads, rivers became the highways for moving goods. The Monongahela River flows from south to north and connects with the Allegheny River to become the Ohio River at Pittsburgh, Pennsylvania. The

 Words to Understand in This Chapter

abolitionist—a person who wanted to abolish, or get rid of, slavery.

auditor—an unbiased person who examines the financial health of an organization.

artifact—an object such as a tool, weapon, or pottery made by people in the past.

treason—the crime of trying to overthrow or harm the government or leaders of one's country.

veneer—a thin layer of high quality wood that is glued onto a piece of lower quality wood.

Ohio River stretches from Pittsburgh to Cairo, Illinois, where it empties into the Mississippi River. Goods can travel by water from West Virginia to New Orleans, Louisiana.

The Potomac River forms part of the border between West Virginia and Maryland. This river empties into the Chesapeake Bay, which connects to the Atlantic Ocean. Other important rivers are the Kanawha, Greenbrier, and Guyandotte.

West Virginia has a four-season climate. The eastern part of the state has warm humid summers and mild winters with occasional snow. The moun-tains are much cooler and may receive heavy snowfall. On average, the state receives about 40 inches (102 cm) of precipitation each year, with the heaviest amounts falling on the western slopes of the highest mountains.

History

The area that is now West Virginia was inhabited long before European settlers arrived. Around 1000 BCE, a group of people called the Adena, or Mound Builders, settled in West Virginia, Kentucky, and Ohio. What we know about them comes from the artifacts found in large mounds where

Barges move coal on the Kanawha River near Charleston. Coal is one of the state's most important natural resources.

Autumn in West Virginia along a mountain stream.

they buried people, tools, and other objects their society valued. One of the largest mounds is Grave Creek Mound. The mound is 69 feet (21 m) tall and 295 feet (90 m) around the base. From the objects in the mounds, it appears that the Adena were farmers and traders.

No one knows why the Adena disappeared, but by the time Europeans arrived in what would become West Virginia, there were only a few Native American villages scattered across the land. However, many tribes such as the Cherokee, Shawnee, Iroquois, and

Delaware claimed the land as their hunting ground.

West Virginia was originally part of the Virginia Colony, but because the mountains were difficult to cross, little was known about the area. In 1671, the Royal Governor of Virginia sent Thomas Batts and Robert Fallam to explore what is now southwest West Virginia. They found a wild land with mink, beaver, and fox. This attracted trappers and traders but few permanent settlers.

Over the next one hundred years, German settlers from Pennsylvania and Maryland spread south down the valleys into what is now northern Virginia and West Virginia. During the French and Indian War (1754–1763) fought between the British and the French over land claims, both sides recruited Native Americans to fight for them. Small settlements in the western part of the state were attacked. Many settlers retreated to British forts for protection.

Once the war ended, more settlers moved west across the mountains. They ignored treaties signed with

Native Americans and settled in what was supposed to be Native American land. Friction between the two groups came to a head in 1774 in a conflict called Lord Dunmore's War. The Native Americans were defeated and forced to give up all claims to the land.

Soldiers from western Virginia fought in the Continental Army during the Revolutionary War, but few battles were fought in this region. After the war, all of the delegates that represented Virginia at the 1787 Constitutional Convention in Philadelphia came from the coastal part of the state, leaving western residents feeling they were not represented.

Western residents felt left out again when Virginia wrote a new constitution in 1829. Only white male landowners would be allowed to vote, and the number of legislators was to be determined by population, with each slave counting as three-fifths of a person. Since settlers in the mountains owned few slaves, this gave all the power to the plantation owners along the coast. Most western Virginia counties voted against this constitu-

Did You Know?

All the Golden Delicious apples in the country trace their roots back to a single tree that grew on a farm in Clay County. The tree and its unusual fruit came to the attention of a nursery that bought the tree and a small amount of ground around it for $5,000 in 1912 (the equivalent of about $120,000 in 2014 dollars). Every year since 1973, Clay County has held the Golden Delicious Festival in September to celebrate the apple.

tion, but it passed anyway.

Many people in the western counties were opposed to slavery. In 1859, an *abolitionist* named John Brown tried to start a slave rebellion in the town of Harpers Ferry on the Potomac River. Brown expected slaves to rise up and join him. This did not happen. Many of Brown's followers were killed and Brown was captured, convicted of *treason* against the state of Virginia, and hanged.

Tensions about slavery boiled over,

and the Civil War began when southern states seceded from the United States to form the Confederate States of America. Virginia was bitterly divided. Virginians who depended on slave labor were in favor of joining the Confederacy. The western counties of Virginia, where slavery was less important, wanted to stay in the Union.

When the Civil War began, the government of Virginia voted to secede from the Union. However, the western counties rejected the idea of leaving the United States. Instead, they voted to break away from Virginia and create a separate state. Legally, a state could not break into smaller states without permission from the state legislature. Leaders of western Virginia argued that since Virginia no longer was part of the United States, they were no longer required to follow that rule.

A series of legal maneuvers began, and once West Virginia agreed to abolish slavery, it was admitted as the thirty-fifth state on June 20, 1863.

Not all West Virginians supported staying in the Union. During the Civil

The front page of a popular magazine from 1859 features a story on the Harper's Ferry insurrection, with an illustration of John Brown.

War, about 30,000 men from West Virginia fought for the Union and about 7,000 for the Confederacy.

After the war ended, Virginia and West Virginia argued over who should pay debts the state had from before the split into two states and where the state boundaries should be. As late as 1991, the two states were still in disagreement over the location of the state borders.

Until the Civil War, rivers had been the main way to get West Virginia's main products—coal, salt, and lumber—to market. After the war, railroads extended into the mountains and provided a new way to ship goods. Eventually railroads linked coal-rich southwestern West Virginia with the port of Hampton Roads on the Virginia coast.

During World War I (1914–1918), the coal industry boomed. Following the war, the United Mine Workers Union attempted to unionize miners to gain better wages and working conditions. Violent strikes set mine owners against workers. In 1921, federal troops had to be brought in to keep order when angry miners fought against state police.

The Great Depression hit West Virginians hard. Many people lost their jobs and struggled to feed their families. Things did not improve until 1941 when the United States entered World War II. Then the coal mines and factories were busy again producing materials needed for the war.

During the 1950s and 1960s, West Virginia's economy went into decline and people moved away look for jobs in other states. Since then, West Virginia has been successful in attracting a variety of businesses that are less dependent on the boom and bust cycle of coal mining.

Government

The government of West Virginia is modeled after the United States government with three branches: executive, legislative, and judicial.

The governor is the chief executive of the state. Governors are elected to four-year terms and may serve only two terms in a row. The governor is responsible for signing or vetoing laws the legislature passes, preparing the state budget, and choosing department heads. Other elected positions in the executive branch include the secretary of state, attorney general, auditor, and treasurer. Unlike many states, West Virginians do not elect a lieu-

Robert Byrd represented West Virginia in the U.S. Senate from 1959 until his death in 2010, making him the longest-serving senator in American history.

tenant governor. The president of the State Senate takes over if the governor dies or is unable to serve.

The legislative branch is made up of the House of Delegates and the Senate. All 100 delegates are elected every two years. The state Senate has 34 members who are elected to four-year terms with half the senators coming up for election every two years. Both the House of Delegates and the Senate must pass a bill before it goes to the governor.

The judicial branch enforces and interprets the state's laws. Magistrates enforce local laws and hear cases involving small amounts of money and minor crimes (misdemeanors). Family courts hear cases involving divorce, child support, and family relationship issues. Circuit courts hear more serious criminal cases (felonies) and cases involving large amounts of money.

The Supreme Court of Appeals is the highest court in the state. Judges for all courts are elected by popular vote. The five Supreme Court justices serve twelve-year terms. Lower court judges serve terms of four to eight years depending on the court.

West Virginia is represented in the United States Congress by three members of the House of Representatives and two Senators, giving the state five electoral votes.

The Economy

West Virginia is rich in natural resources. In the 1800s, the state exported coal, salt, and lumber. Today salt is no longer mined in quantity, but coal mining and timber are still important to the state's economy.

About 80 percent of West Virginia, or 12 million acres, is covered with forests. These forests make West Virginia one of the top wood-producing states in the nation. Each year, its forests provide 700 million board feet of lumber, 800 million square feet of *veneer*, and 770 million square feet of a particle-board like material used in construction.

Coal was discovered in West Virginia in 1742. It can be found in 53 of the state's 55 counties, giving West Virginia 4 percent of all the coal reserves in the United States. Today, active mining takes place in more than half of West Virginia's counties.

Coal mining is a dirty, dangerous job. In the first half of the 1900s, miners fought for safer working conditions, better pay, and the right to join the United Mine Workers union. Their strikes often resulted in violence. Today conditions at the mines have improved, although mine deaths still occur. In April 2010, for example, 29 miners were killed in an explosion in Raleigh County.

Chemical manufacturing is also a major part of West Virginia's economy. More than 140 companies employ 12,800 individuals in chemical production. Large companies such as Dow, DuPont, and BASF have manu-

West Virginia accounts for about 12 percent of the total U.S. coal production each year, more than any state except Wyoming.

facturing plants in the state.

Critics have accused chemical companies of polluting West Virginia's rivers and streams. In one notable incident, a chemical leak into the Elk River in Charleston left about 300,000 residents of central West Virginia unable to use the drinking water for several weeks in January 2014. The state is working with chemical companies to make sure its waterways and sources of drinking water are safe to use.

A clean environment is important to the tourism industry in West

The state capitol building in Charleston houses the West Virginia legislature as well as the governor's office. The building was opened in 1932.

Virginia. The forests and mountains attract hikers, hunters, fishermen, and whitewater canoeists. Millions of visitors come to West Virginia each year.

Other large employers include the government, health and education services, and professional and business services. The state has about 21,500 farms. Beef cattle, eggs, and corn are the most commonly produced products.

Compared to other states, West Virginia is a poor state. According to the U.S. Census Bureau, the median household income is about $40,400, almost $13,000 less than the national median income. In 2013, 17.6 percent of residents had an income that fell below the federal poverty level. This was higher than the national average of 14.9 percent.

The People

In the census of 1800, the part of Virginia that is now West Virginia had about 203,518 residents of which only 23,597 were slaves. This compares to the rest of Virginia where almost half the population were slaves. By 2015, the state's population had grown to over 1.85 million.

The population of West Virginia has little diversity. Almost 94 percent of the population self-identifies as white. This includes 1.4 percent who also identify as Hispanic or Latino. Blacks or African Americans make up 3.6 percent of the population, with only about 2 percent of people representing all other races combined. Only 1.4 percent of the population was born in a foreign country and only 2.4 percent speak a language other than English at home. This compares to 12.9 percent

Three federal interstate highways converge at Charleston, the capital and largest city in West Virginia.

foreign-born residents and 20.5 percent of home speakers of another language in the nation as a whole.

Only 35 percent of people in West Virginia say they actively practice a religion compared to 49 percent in the nation as a whole. Of those who are religions, most are Protestants. Of these, the Baptists and Methodists are the largest denominations. Only about 5 percent of the population is Catholic, and Latter Day Saints (Mormons), Jews, or Muslims each represent less than 1 percent of the religious population.

People in West Virginia graduate from high school at only a slightly lower rate than the rest of the country (83.4 percent vs. 85.7 percent), but many fewer of them earn college degrees (17.9 percent vs. a national average of 28.5 percent). The state has a higher rate of home ownership than much of the rest of the country, but the value of homes is much lower than the national average.

Major Cities

The major cities in West Virginia are all located on rivers. Cities grew up along waterways because during the colonial era, the rivers provided the cheapest and easiest way to transport people and goods. *Charleston*, the largest city in West Virginia, is the only city in the state with a population of more than 50,000. Charleston is located where the Elk and Kanawha Rivers meet. Three interstate highways also meet in Charleston, making

Some Famous West Virginians

West Virginia is a small state, but it has produced some famous people. General Chuck Yeager (b. 1923) of Hamlin joined U.S. Army Air Force and flew combat missions during World War II. When the war ended, he became a test pilot. Yeager was the first person to fly faster than the speed of sound and went on to break many speed and altitude records.

Astronaut Jon McBride (b. 1943), born in Charleston but raised in Beckley, piloted the Space Shuttle *Challenger*, which launched on October 5, 1984, on an eight-day mission. A NASA facility in Fairmont is named for him.

Chuck Yeager

Brad Paisley (b. 1972) of Glen Dale has won just about every country music award there is more than once. He began performing at age ten and started writing songs three years later. Between 1999 and 2014, he released ten albums.

Other famous West Virginians include Nobel Prize winning author Pearl Buck (1892–1973). Buck was born in Hillsboro but lived most of her life in China. Her best-known book was *The Good Earth*. In 1984, Mary Lou Retton (b. 1966) of Fairmont was the first American woman to win an Olympic gold medal in the all-around gymnastics category. Bill Mazeroski (b. 1936) the great defensive second baseman for the Pittsburgh Pirates from 1956 to 1972, was inducted into the Baseball Hall of Fame in 2001.

Brad Paisley

it a land, as well as a river, transportation hub. Since Charleston is the state capital, government is one of the largest employers.

Huntington is located in the southwest corner of West Virginia where West Virginia, Ohio, and Kentucky come together and where the Guyandotte and Ohio Rivers meet. It is the largest inland port in the United States in terms of tons of goods shipped. Coal is one of the major products shipped from Huntington. Huntington was originally a manufacturing city, but in the 1970s, manufacturing jobs moved elsewhere. Today the city is reinventing itself as a center of education and medical care. Marshall University is the city's largest employer. The online store Amazon.com opened a large customer service center in the city in 2011.

Parkersburg, the third-largest city in West Virginia, is north of Huntington where the Little Kanawha River flows into the Ohio River.

Smaller towns of interest in West Virginia include *Harpers Ferry*, the site of John Brown's failed slave revolt; *Shepherdstown*, the oldest settlement in the state; and *Moundsville*, site of the Grave Creek Mound.

Further Reading

Casto, James E. *Southern West Virginia: Coal Country*. Charleston, S.C.: Arcadia, 2004.

Field, Ron. *Avenging Angel: John Brown's Raid on Harpers Ferry 1859*. Botley, Oxford, UK: Osprey Publishing, 2012.

Gaffney, Timothy. *Chuck Yeager: First Man to Fly Faster Than Sound*. Chicago: Children's Press, 1986.

Petreycik, Rick. *West Virginia*. New York: Cavendish Square Publishers, 2014.

Steelhammer, Rick. *It Happened in West Virginia: Remarkable Events that Shaped History*. Guilford, Conn.: Globe Pequot Press, 2013.

Williams, Colleen. *Chuck Yeager*. Philadelphia: Chelsea House, 2003.

Internet Resources

www.wvculture.org/history/archivesindex.aspx

The West Virginia History Archives have links to online primary sources, lesson plans, and resources for each West Virginia county.

www.wvculture.org/history/timetrl/timetrl.html

Two-minute radio broadcasts about historical events in West Virginia produced by West Virginia Public Radio are available at this site.

www.wvtourism.com

Official tourism site for the state of West Virginia.

http://www.wvcommerce.org

The West Virginia Department of Commerce provides this page with links to tourism, natural resources, energy, the workforce, and people & places.

 # Text-Dependent Questions

1. Why were rivers so important to the development of West Virginia?
2. What were some of the reasons West Virginia separated from Virginia during the Civil War?
3. Name three important industries in West Virginia today.

 # Research Project

In 1920, the United Mine Workers of America (UMWA) tried to unionize miners in Mingo and Logan Counties against the wishes of the mine owners. There were violent confrontations and on May 21, 1921, West Virginia Governor E. F. Morgan declared a state of war in Mingo County. Research what happened at this miner's revolt called Blood Mingo, and write a short paper on how the conflict ended.

Index

Numbers in **bold italics** refer to captions.

Series Glossary of Key Terms

bicameral—having two legislative chambers (for example, a senate and a house of representatives).

cede—to yield or give up land, usually through a treaty or other formal agreement.

census—an official population count.

constitution—a written document that embodies the rules of a government.

delegation—a group of persons chosen to represent others.

elevation—height above sea level.

legislature—a lawmaking body.

precipitation—rain and snow.

term limit—a legal restriction on how many consecutive terms an office holder may serve.